HOLOCAUST BIOGRAPHIES

Mordechai Anielewicz

Hero of the Warsaw Ghetto Uprising

Kerry P. Callahan

THE ROSEN PUBLISHING GROUP, INC.
NEW YORK

For my parents

Published in 2001 by The Rosen Publishing Group, Inc.
29 East 21st Street, New York, NY 10010

Copyright © 2001 by The Rosen Publishing Group, Inc.

First Edition

Library of Congress Cataloging-in-Publication Data

Callahan, Kerry P.
Mordechai Anielewicz: hero of the Warsaw ghetto uprising / Kerry P. Callahan.
p. cm. — (Holocaust biographies)
Includes bibliographical references and index.
ISBN 0-8239-3377-6 (library binding)
1. Anielewicz, Mordechai, 1919–1943—Juvenile literature.
2. Jews—Poland—Warsaw—Biography—Juvenile literature.
3. Warsaw (Poland)—Biography—Juvenile literature.
4. Holocaust, Jewish (1939–1945)—Poland—Warsaw—
Biography—Juvenile literature. 5. Warsaw (Poland)—History—
Warsaw Ghetto Uprising, 1943—Juvenile literature.
[1. Anielewicz, Mordechai, 1919–1943. 2. Jews—Poland—Warsaw.
3. Holocaust, Jewish (1939–1945)—Poland—Warsaw. 4. Warsaw
(Poland)—History—Warsaw Ghetto Uprising, 1943.]
I. Title. II. Series.
DS135.P63 A6625 2001
943.8'4—dc21

                                                           2001000515

Manufactured in the United States of America

Contents

Introduction 5

1. Little Angel 11

2. Hitler's Racial World Order 23

3. Hitler's Plans for Poland 31

4. The Jewish Community 42

5. The Warsaw Ghetto 53

6. Deportations 67

7. The First Uprising 80

8. The Final Uprising 89

Timeline 102

Glossary 104

For More Information 107

For Further Reading 109

Index 110

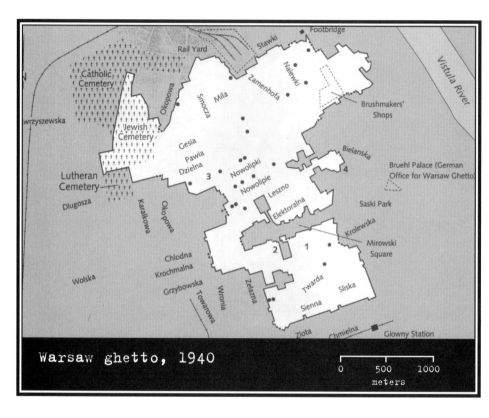

Warsaw ghetto, 1940

0   500   1000
meters

- Ghetto boundary, November 15, 1940: wall with barbed wire
- Entrances, gates to ghetto
- Selected ghetto factories

1. Jewish Council (Judenrat)
2. Jewish police
3. Hiding Place of Ringelblum Archice
4. The Great Synagogue

Map labels: Footbridge, Rail Yard, Stawki, Catholic Cemetery, Nalewki, Vistula River, Okopowa, Mila, Zamenhofa, Smocza, Jewish Cemetery, wrzyszewska, Brushmakers' Shops, Gesia, Pawia, Dzielna, Bielanska, Lutheran Cemetery, Dlugosza, Karalkowa, Oko powa, Nowolipki, Nowolipie, Leszno, 3, 4, Bruehl Palace (German Office for Warsaw Ghetto), Saski Park, Elektoralna, Krolewska, Chlodna, Krochmalna, Wolska, Grzybowska, Towarowa, Wronia, Zelazna, 2, 1, Twarda, Sliska, Mirowski Square, Sienna, Zlota, Chmielna, Glowny Station

Introduction

April 23, 1943
Peace go with you, my friend! Perhaps we may still meet again! The dream of my life has risen to become fact. Self-defense in the ghetto will have been a reality. Jewish armed resistance and revenge are facts. I have been a witness to the magnificent, heroic fighting of Jewish men of battle.

> —Mordechai Anielewicz, in a letter to his friend, Yitzhak Cukierman

Mordechai Anielewicz wrote these words at the age of twenty-four, revealing the passion and courage that defined his all-too-brief life. As Anielewicz lived much of his life figuratively—and sometimes literally—underground, we still know relatively little about him. Yet, his work as a young Zionist, peaceful protestor, and armed freedom fighter provides us with a rich time capsule, one that displays the political complexity and cultural depth of Eastern European Jewry in the first half of the twentieth century.

An activist within the Jewish community in Poland before the outbreak of World War II, Anielewicz went on to organize and lead the historic Warsaw ghetto uprising. This uprising was the single largest armed Jewish resistance against the Nazis during the war. Anielewicz and the small band of fighters he commanded believed that, even in the face of overwhelming odds, Jews living in Warsaw should fight Nazi tyranny to the bitter end. The significance of their stand cannot be overstated. To all who survived the Holocaust, as well as to those of us who still seek to understand it generations later, their resistance remains a powerful symbol of courage.

Applauding the uprising should not imply that armed resistance was the only or preferred way to respond to Nazi brutality. The Holocaust was a uniquely horrifying event. In Germany and other Nazi-occupied countries, Nazis isolated Jews from the rest of the population and earmarked them for total destruction. The Nazis built death camps equipped with the most sophisticated technology available. They systematically rounded up and murdered approximately 6 million Jews, including 1.5 million Jewish children and teenagers.

Genocide, or the deliberate destruction of people of one ethnic, political, or cultural group, had occurred prior to the Holocaust. But, Adolf Hitler, dictator of Germany from 1933 until his death in 1945, defined his victims racially. More specifically, Hitler's hateful worldview defined being Jewish as a racial identity, not simply a religious or cultural one. Hitler not only claimed that Jews constituted a distinct race of people but also that they were biologically inferior.

Hitler's army invaded Poland on September 1, 1939, starting World War II. On September 28, the Polish army surrendered the capital, Warsaw. When the German army invaded Poland, few realized the extent of Hitler's plans to commit racial genocide. Hitler's plans were far-reaching and eerily systematic. The Nazis sought to eliminate what they defined as the "Jewish race" in its entirety.

The German program for Polish Jews was one of concentration, isolation, and ultimately, annihilation. The Nazis forced Jews living in rural areas to move into overcrowded urban centers. They isolated Jews from the rest of Polish society. In several Polish cities, including Warsaw, they sealed Jews in ghettos, walled-off cities within cities. Within these ghettos, conditions were miserable; residents sorely lacked food, heat, water, housing, and health care.

Despite the violent tactics of the Nazis, many Jews initially hoped that they could endure until the end of the war. Jews throughout Eastern Europe had long confronted anti-Semitism, especially in the form of violent pogroms. Local non-Jewish officials often encouraged these organized attacks against Jews that frequently resulted in destruction of property, physical injury, and sometimes death. Consequently, some Jews viewed Nazi tactics as yet another wave of violent anti-Semitism, not unlike that experienced by prior generations.

During World War II, as evidence of the systematic mass murder of Jews surfaced, it became clear that Jews could in no way appease German authorities. Nothing—not offers of labor, services, goods, or money—could guarantee one's safety. Suddenly, hope for a Jewish legacy was running out. In the face of this deliberate and powerful evil, was resistance futile? The life and death of Mordechai Anielewicz answers with a resounding "No."

One of 350,000 Jews imprisoned by the Germans in the Warsaw ghetto, Anielewicz was only twenty-three years old when he became commander of the Jewish Combat Organization (*Zydowska Organizacja Bjowa*), or ZOB. The ZOB attempted to stop the Nazis from completing the final deportation of Jews in Warsaw to concentration or death camps. Small organized and armed fighting units forced the Germans to deploy a substantial military force and engage in prolonged combat.

Unfortunately, the Nazis did ultimately subdue the ZOB. Those who were not killed in battle either committed suicide or were captured and sent to concentration camps.

Like many of his comrades, Commander Anielewicz died in battle on May 8, 1943. His story, though, is not only one of death but also of life. His life gives us valuable insight into what it meant to be young, Jewish, and politically active in Poland between the world wars. Perhaps most important, his story gives voice to Jews, imprisoned within ghetto walls during the Holocaust, who fought annihilation.

1. Little Angel

In 1919, at the conclusion of World War I, Allied powers—primarily Britain, France, the United States, and Italy—drafted the Treaty of Versailles. Germany signed the treaty, which was one of several created at the Paris peace conference resulting in the international settlement of the war. In many ways, the Treaty of Versailles restructured Europe. In particular, it called for the creation of the republic of Poland.

Participants in the peace conference understood that Poland had a culturally diverse population with a greater number of minorities than any other European state, except Russia. In fact, over three million Jews lived in Poland, constituting almost 10 percent of the general population. Consequently, participants in the

Officials leave the Palace of Versailles in
France after signing the Treaty of Versailles
on June 28, 1919.

Paris peace conference also wrote the Minority Treaty, wherein Polish representatives guaranteed a number of minority rights. They pledged to ensure the civil and political equality of minorities, to safeguard their rights as citizens, and to extend to all minorities the right to establish their own educational, religious, charitable, and social institutions. Polish representatives accepted and signed the Minority Treaty as part of the overall peace treaty on June 28, 1919.

That same year, Mordechai Anielewicz was born in Warsaw, the Polish capital and home to over 350,000 Jews. Like many other Jewish families in Poland at that time, the Anielewicz family was quite poor. A worldwide economic depression in the 1920s and 1930s and the active anti-Semitic policies of the Polish government combined to keep the overall economic level of the Jewish community low.

Except for a small number of wealthy and upper-middle-class Jews, the majority were lower-middle-class workers, small business owners, or unemployed. Discriminatory university admissions policies further aggravated these economic conditions. Anti-Semitism also limited Jews' access to professional work.

Polish Jews confronted many other forms of discrimination as well. Despite the promises of the Minority Treaty signed only a decade earlier, in the 1930s the Polish government enacted a torrent of anti-Semitic legislation. These laws often characterized Jews who had long populated towns and villages across Poland as outsiders. In fact, the national government went so far as to institute an official policy of evacuating Jews from Poland. In 1938, the Polish government revoked the citizenship of Polish Jews living abroad. Jews living in Poland also faced pogroms. Derived from a Ukranian word meaning "to wreak havoc," pogroms were the periodic attacks against Jews, when angry mobs terrorized their communities, assaulted residents, and destroyed property.

Hard Times

Historian Joseph Tenenbaum, in his 1930 address to the National Convention of the American Jewish Congress in Washington, DC, explained how discrimination aggravated the economic condition of Jews in Poland:

"The position of the Jews in Poland is untenable and disastrous, so heart-rending, indeed, that no words can picture adequately the misery, the utter despair, the hopelessness of the Jewish masses in Poland. Of the three million Jews, at least two million are hovering on the brink of starvation. Discrimination and the systematic elimination of the Jews from the economic life of the country . . . the spread of monopolies with the virtual exclusion of the Jews from their operations, state protectionism applied to non-Jewish enterprises, are cutting at the root of Jewish production. The Sunday blue laws, indirectly compelling Jews to cease work for two and a half days in the week; limitations or exclusion of Jews from government and municipal offices and establishments, and other measures of that nature, have succeeded in undermining the basic structure of Jewish economic life in Poland."

Despite the economic, legislative, and violent anti-Semitism Jews in Poland encountered, Mordechai Anielewicz came of age within a community rich in religious and cultural tradition. Observant Jews in Poland accounted for half, perhaps more, of eastern European Jewry (except Russia) before World War II. The observance of Judaism permeated all aspects of public Jewish life. Most Jews kept the Sabbath as a day of rest and abstained from traditionally forbidden foods. Judaism was practiced in thousands of formal and informal groups: synagogues, houses of prayer and houses of study, ritual baths and ritual slaughter, religious courts, congregational bodies, women's organizations, publishing houses, and presses. From these shared religious and cultural spaces grew a vast network of educational and charitable institutions.

But Jewish life in prewar Poland was also undergoing a swift secularization. Especially among the younger generation, politics began to take precedence over religion. In the face of the unfair treatment Jews faced, many young people began to organize politically radical antireligious groups that focused on remedying the plight of Jews in eastern Europe. One such institution, the Zionist youth movement, played a particularly pivotal role in the life of Mordechai Anielewicz.

The Zionist Youth Movement

Zionism stems in part from the ancient religious attachment of Jews and the Jewish religion to the historical region of Palestine, home of a hill in ancient Jerusalem called Zion. Palestine is known as *Eretz Yisra'el,* or "the Land of Israel" in Hebrew. Zionism began as a political movement in eastern and central Europe in the latter part of the nineteenth century. Faced with exclusion and anti-Semitism, Jewish leaders discussed the need for a national sense of identity among Jews. Zionists called for the creation of a Jewish national state in Palestine. Theodor Herzl, who

some consider the father of political Zionism,
outlined his vision for a Jewish state in his
book *The Jewish State*, in February 1896:

> I consider the Jewish question neither a
> social nor a religious one, even though it
> sometimes takes these and other forms.
> It is a national question, and to solve it
> we must first of all establish it as an
> international problem to be discussed
> and settled by the civilized nations of
> the world in council. We are a people—
> one people. We have sincerely tried
> everywhere to merge with the national
> communities in which we live, seeking
> only to preserve the faith of our fathers.
> It is not permitted us. In vain we are
> loyal patriots, sometimes superloyal. In
> our native lands where we have lived for
> centuries we are still decried as aliens,
> often by men whose ancestors had not
> yet come at a time when Jewish sighs
> had long been heard in the country . . .

Many Jews, liberal and conservative, religious and secular, joined the Zionist movement. The Zionist youth movement consisted of a number of different youth groups with varying political and cultural agendas, each providing an opportunity for teenagers to put their feelings and ideals into action and impact the world around them.

Most of these groups stressed education, studying Hebrew and the geography of Palestine, vocational training, and immigration to Palestine as goals for their members. These groups also enabled young people to connect and organize with others who held similar ideals. As a social and political force within the Jewish community, they were quite effective. In terms of community organization, education, and political action, their influence greatly exceeded their numbers.

After finishing secondary school, where he earned the nickname Aniolek, or "little angel," Anielewicz joined the Zionist youth

Mordechai Anielewicz stands at the right in this
group portrait of members of Hashomer Hatzair,
taken in Warsaw, Poland, in 1938.

group Hashomer Hatzair. Still an active organization, Hashomer Hatzair was founded in eastern Europe on the eve of World War I. In its early stages, Hashomer Hatzair was heavily influenced by the scout movement and embraced scouting as a way to teach youth self-reliance, outdoor life, and a love and knowledge of nature. Further, leaders hoped to foster a sense of independence and creativity among their membership.

Politically, Hashomer Hatzair began as a Zionist-socialist pioneering movement whose aim was to educate Jewish youth for life in a future Jewish state. To that end, members gained experience working on communal farms known as kibbutzim. As socialists, the group stressed the need for Jewish people to become workers and farmers who would settle in the Land of Israel. Ultimately, they dreamt of creating a society based on social justice and equality in their new homeland.

Anielewicz soon became a leader within Hashomer Hatzair, whose ranks numbered 70,000 worldwide on the eve of World War II. Like many of his fellow members, Anielewicz led community-building projects. He helped establish schools, cultural facilities, a publishing house, a daily newspaper, and agricultural colonies.

By 1939, Anielewicz was teaching at the agricultural colony located in Wloclawek, Poland. He then traveled with other members of the agricultural school to Wilno to await transportation of his wards to Palestine. He himself did not remain in Wilno but returned to Warsaw, where his skills as an organizer and leader would soon prove invaluable.

2. Hitler's Racial World Order

As Anielewicz continued his work with Hashomer Hatzair, the German army invaded Poland. This attack on September 1, 1939, set World War II in motion. On September 17, the Soviet army invaded Poland from the east. Overwhelmed, the ill-prepared Polish army surrendered by early October. The exiled Polish government regrouped in London, where it would remain in close contact with underground resistance groups throughout the war.

Although it was no secret that vicious anti-Semitism formed the cornerstone of Nazi racial ideology, and, consequently, wartime policy, few realized the extent of Nazi plans for the destruction of European Jewry at the outset of World War II. Hitler and high-ranking Nazi officials had discussed a number of strategies for realizing a Nazi racial world order. In fact, the notion of race was at the center of National Socialist ideology and the platform on which both Hitler and his party came to power.

The Third Reich (empire), the official Nazi designation for Hitler's regime, controlled Germany from January 1933 until May 1945. Hitler became chancellor of Germany on January 30, 1933. After President Paul von Hindenburg's death, Hitler assumed the twin titles of leader (Führer) and chancellor on August 2, 1934. This step solidified his position as dictator of Germany; it was also the culmination of a political journey begun a decade earlier.

Hitler had become actively interested in German politics at the end of World War I. A highly decorated soldier, lauded for his courage and skill during the war, he was infuriated by the terms of the Paris peace settlement. He denounced it as intolerable and argued that the terms of the peace treaty unnecessarily punished Germany for World War I. In September 1919,

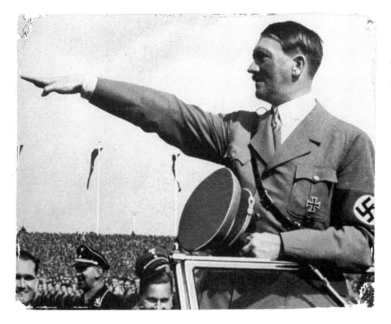

Hitler solidified his position as dictator of Germany in August 1934.

while still active in the German army, Hitler joined the German Workers' Party in Munich. In 1920, party leaders put Hitler in charge of party propaganda. Soon after, Hitler left the army to fully devote himself to politics. Specifically, he hoped to garner further support for the party, which in that year was renamed the *National-Sozialistische Deutsche Arbeiterpartei*, or the Nazi Party.

Deteriorating economic and social conditions rendered Germany ripe for the development of such a party. The loss of World War I and the terms of the Treaty of Versailles, especially the payment of war reparations, hurt an already devastated German economy. These terms fueled German anger and brought about widespread discontent with the national government, known as the Weimar Republic.

As the public's frustration increased, so too did the popularity of the Nazi Party. Hitler took advantage of the prevailing lawlessness and opposition to the Weimar Republic in November 1923. In an armed takeover, Hitler and party members took government officials hostage in Munich and forced them to proclaim a national revolution. When released, however, the officials reversed their proclamation. Hitler was arrested and sentenced to five years in prison. As it turned out, he only served nine months, and in relative comfort, at that.

Mein Kampf

While in prison, Hitler wrote *Mein Kampf* (My Struggle), an autobiography that would become the Nazi Party manual. In *Mein Kampf,* Hitler documented his racist, anti-Semitic ideology. He argued that race, or the biological inheritance of physical and cultural traits, defined human existence. The racial question "gives the key not only to world history, but to all human culture," for, he believed, "in the blood alone resides the strength as well as the weakness of man." In Hitler's mind, the world was made up of races of people, or people of the same "blood," who competed for territory and power. He surmised that only the fittest survived; maintaining racial purity was the key to survival. Only "pure" races that did not mix with "inferior" groups created civilized societies.

Hitler also explained his intensely hateful worldview in more specific terms: Among the "white race," the "Aryans" formed the elite. In Hitler's mind, the Aryan race held the key to

human cultural development. Hitler believed
that the very existence of world civilization
depended on maintaining and safeguarding
the purity of the Aryan race. Aryans were
destined to rule and enslave inferior races.
One of these inferior races was the Jews. Hitler
argued that since the dawn of time, Aryans
and Jews had been adversaries.

A 1924 advertisement for *Mein Kampf*

To Hitler, the "Jew" was the complete opposite of the Aryan. In his system, Aryans represented the supreme perfection of human existence, whereas the Jews embodied evil. He wrote, "the 'vileness' of the Jew is so gigantic that no one need be surprised if among our people the personification of the Devil as the symbol of all evil assumes the living shape of the Jews." The "vileness" of the Jew, Hitler claimed, resided in the blood of the race and was thereby evident in the Jew's physical, mental, and cultural being. Further, Hitler argued that this vileness had already infected nearly every aspect of modern society.

Hitler's elaborate doctrines of race culminated in his foreign policy program for a National Socialist Germany, for he believed that the state existed merely as a means to an end: the preservation of the racial community. As dictator, with iron-fisted control over German society and a fiercely loyal and highly trained military force under his command, Hitler planned to realize his racial vision in the name of the Aryan race. With the invasion of Poland, Hitler acquired the land and resources necessary to expand his war effort. In Poland, he also intended to reinvent civilization according to his own horrifying vision of racial world order.

3. Hitler's Plans for Poland

On September 28, 1939, Germany and Russia partitioned Poland; Germany seized the western territories, and Russia the eastern areas. The Germans divided their territory by annexing, or incorporating, land along the German border. The other portion became a German protectorate (area under German rule) known as the *Generalgouvernement.* With this occupation of Poland, Adolf Hitler had the opportunity to carry out his deadly racial agenda. As World War II unfolded, the fate of Jews throughout Europe depended upon each country's wartime relationship with Germany. Where German rule was total and supreme, Jews eventually would face annihilation. In the Generalgouvernement, the Jews came under the direct authority of a governor appointed by Hitler and the *Schutzstaffel* (SS).

The SS came into being early in 1925. Drawn from the ranks of the Nazi Party, SS members served as bodyguards for the party's leadership. Significantly, the SS swore allegiance not to Germany but to Adolf Hitler. Heinrich Himmler, a German National Socialist politician, police administrator, and military commander, headed the organization. He soon became the second most powerful man in the Third Reich. During the war, Himmler was intimately involved in orchestrating and implementing the Nazis' plans for Poland.

Soon after Germany invaded Poland, Hitler issued a decree establishing a civil administration within the General-gouvernement. German civil authorities governed the area, led by the iron fist of Hans Frank. The Generalgouvernement was to serve as a dumping ground for Poles, Jews, and non-Jews expelled from the part of Poland that Germany had annexed. The total number of people involved in the population transfer has been estimated at one million.

Governor Hans Frank (left) hosts SS head Heinrich Himmler (right) at Wewel Castle during Himmler's visit to Krakow, Poland, in 1940.

As soon as the German army invaded Poland, Hitler, Himmler, and other Nazi leaders ordered the rank and file to execute thousands of non-Jewish Poles. While the Nazis reserved their deepest hatred for Jews, characterizing them as evil embodied, they regarded non-Jewish Poles as racially beneath them: subhuman. Consequently, during the first months of the invasion, Germany eliminated the Polish elite. The Germans killed tens of thousands of non-Jewish Polish intellectuals, including many teachers and religious leaders. They sent thousands to Germany as slave laborers, while many others were transported into the Generalgouvernement.

Segregation

Historians continue to debate precisely when Hitler and the Nazi Party elite decided upon a policy of total destruction of European Jewry. The Nazi plan for genocide most likely resulted from a chain of political and bureaucratic decisions made between September 1939 and the late fall of 1941. In a memo dated September 21, 1939, just weeks after the German army invaded Poland, Reinhard Heydrich, Himmler's chief lieutenant and head of the Reich security main office recorded Nazi plans:

I refer to the conference held in Berlin today, and again point out that the planned total measures (i.e., the final aim—*Endziel*) are to be kept strictly secret. A distinction must be made between:

1. The final aim (which will require extended periods of time)

2. The stages leading to the final aim which will be carried out in short periods

Heydrich emphasized the need to perform these measures in stages so as not to arouse suspicion of their final aim. His use of the term "final aim" eerily foreshadows the Final Solution. The Final Solution was the code name for the Nazi plan to destroy the Jews. Ominously vague, this memo also illustrates the degree to which it was difficult for many to discern Nazi intentions.

In another memo, Heydrich outlined the first order of business: "For the time being, the first prerequisite for the final aim is the concentration of the Jews from the countryside into the larger cities." This was one of the many measures that served to physically, socially, and legally fabricate the racial categories of Aryans and Jews. While Himmler was ultimately accountable for this program, Heydrich and his *Einsatzgruppen* (special-duty groups) would execute the process. The Einsatzgruppen was a mobile paramilitary police force that would provide a strike force for the police and security intelligence. Their sadistic atrocities against Jews shocked even some army generals.

Within the first few months of the occupation, the Nazis destroyed thousands of Jewish settlements. They expelled Jews from towns and villages throughout Poland and sent them to nearby cities. They forced Jews from their homes and forbade them to take bare necessities. Jews were condemned to exposure, hunger, and homelessness. The Jewish

Identifying Marks for Jews in the Government-General, November 23, 1939

Regulation for the Identification of Jewish Men and Women in the Government-General, November 23, 1939

§ 1

All Jews and Jewesses within the Government-General who are over ten years of age are required, beginning December 1, 1939, to wear on the right sleeve of their inner and outer garments a white band at least ten cm wide, with the Star of David on it.

§ 2

Jews and Jewesses must procure these armbands themselves, and provide them with the required distinguishing mark.

§ 3

1) Violations will be punished by imprisionment.

2) Cases will be judged by Special Courts.

§ 4

Orders required for the implementation of this regulation will be issued by the Chief of the Internal Administration Division in the Governor General's office.

Cracow, November 23, 1939
The Governor General for the Occupied Polish Territories Frank

population was concentrated in a few urban areas within the Generalgouvernement, so the Nazis segregated Jews from the rest of the population. Their separation was the first step in the plan to annihilate them.

Governor Frank issued a dizzying series of ordinances whose purpose was also to isolate Jewish Poles from non-Jewish Poles and subject them to special treatment. Nazis randomly seized Jews and sent them to forced labor camps. Jews were forbidden access to certain sections of the city; they were allotted smaller food rations than the non-Jewish Poles. They were forbidden to work in key industries in government offices, or even to bake bread.

Laws also forbade Jews from buying from or selling goods to Aryans, from receiving treatment from Aryan doctors, from tending to Aryan sick, from riding trains and trolley cars, from leaving the city limits without special permits, and from possessing gold or jewelry. From December 1939 onward, every Jew ten years of age or older was compelled to

Jewish leaders meet to protest the Nazi regime's
anti-Jewish legislation in Warsaw.

wear an armband with a Star of David printed
on it. Failure to obey any of these regulations
usually resulted in death, but even careful
obedience to the rules did not protect against
violence and degradation.

All over Poland, synagogues went up in
flames. The Nazis had deemed the entire
public existence of the religious community
illegal and the observant were singled out for

persecution. All functions pertaining to the observance of Judaism—public and/or private worship, religious study, and religious teaching—were outlawed.

Terror enveloped the Jews. Unbridled killing and senseless violence became daily occurrences. The fear of sudden death became normal. In many places, the Nazis organized pogroms, rounding up the non-Jewish Polish population to help mock, abuse, injure, and murder Jews.

Within this chaotic and violent environment, Mordechai Anielewicz remained a loyal and steadfast community leader and protestor. Anielewicz organized resistance groups to stop pogrom gangs that invaded Jewish neighborhoods and communities. Like many within the Jewish community at that time, Anielewicz found his role as community leader and activist transformed during World War II.

Prior to the war, organizations such as Hashomer Hatzair offered members a sense of cultural identity and belonging that helped relieve the effects of anti-Semitism. In response to the German invasion and the Nazis' increasingly harsh treatment, Jewish organizations, including those within the Zionist movement, began to focus on resistance. The seeds of resistance are evident in this article from an underground newspaper, *Youth Speaks*:

> If in the years before the war education within the Movement was directed towards the pioneering effort in Eretz Israel, then at this time we must emphasize that in the education of the youth we must combine the demand for pioneering effort in Eretz Israel with the need to be active here, in order that we may stand fast, and exist and remain alive.

Indeed, like Anielewicz, many young Jews in Poland plotted against the Nazis at every turn.

4. The Jewish Community

On November 28, 1939, Governor Frank issued a decree ordering the formation in each city of a *Judenrat*, or Jewish council, composed of leaders from within the Jewish community. Frank's orders specified that the Judenrat would accept and enforce all German orders. His order also stipulated that Jews must obey the Judenrat. According to Frank:

> It is the duty of the Judenrat through its chairman or his deputy to receive the orders of the German administration. It is responsible for carrying out of orders to their full extent. The directives it issues to carry out these German decrees must be obeyed by all Jews and Jewesses.

From the very first day of its establishment, Judenrats officially governed the Jewish community within each city. To further secure order, each Judenrat eventually organized a uniformed police force. Overseen by the Judenrats, the Jewish police sought to protect the Jewish community and enforce German orders. These conflicting loyalties soon took their toll on police officers. Initially, some police officers did attempt to remain community minded. Before long, though, the Germans weeded out those officers who acted on behalf of the Jews. As Jews began to distrust the Jewish police, officers asserted their authority with increasing force. Rather than being protectors, they became yet another enemy.

The leadership role played by the Judenrats also developed under contradictory pressures. On the one hand, the Judenrats enforced German orders, but on the other, they hoped to meet the needs of the Jewish community. Although ultimately they acted as agents of the Germans, the Judenrats saw themselves as comforters of the Jews. Initially, members of each Judenrat hoped to serve as a buffer insulating the Jewish community from Nazis.

For instance, in Warsaw, shortly after the occupation, Germans randomly captured Jews on the street and sent them to forced labor camps. In these camps, prisoners worked under horrendous conditions; SS soldiers often shot or beat workers to death. In an effort to lessen the

German police inspect the papers of a Jewish man in Warsaw.

terrorizing effect this had, the Warsaw Judenrat
organized a labor pool. From this pool, the
Judenrat sought to supply the Germans with the
workers they demanded. In this way, the
Judenrat attempted to control the movement of
Jews into labor camps. The hope was that this
would enable Jews in Warsaw to move about
more freely, assured that they would not be
kidnapped if they went out for bread or to work.

As conditions in the labor camps were often
deadly, some Jews ignored Judenrat orders and
refused to go. But the fact remained that the
Warsaw Judenrat needed to provide the
Germans with a certain number of workers. As a
result, the Judenrat became increasingly
forceful. They feared that unless workers came
forward, both the Judenrat and the Jewish
community would suffer terrible consequences.
The Judenrat's role in supplying forced labor
soon came to be resented by Warsaw Jews. It
became only another means of appeasing the
Germans. It also became clear that since the
Judenrat took their orders from the Germans,

their ability to ease the plight of Warsaw Jews was severely compromised.

Further complicating the Jews' helpless position was the unwritten but well-understood law of collective responsibility. Of the many rules and regulations imposed by the Germans, this was one of the most harmful. The rebellious act of one person often resulted in the punishment of many. As one Warsaw inhabitant noted:

> Thus, in the first days of November 1939, fifty-three male inhabitants of the 9 Nalewki Street apartment house were summarily shot for the beating of a Polish policeman by one of the tenants. This occurrence, the first case of mass punishment, intensified the feeling of panic amongst the Warsaw Jews.

The Germans applied this law universally against the Jews. The assignment of collective responsibility put intense pressure upon the Jewish community.

This was one reason why individual acts of resistance, let alone organizing a resistance movement, seemed at best unwise and at worst irresponsible to many community elders. By resisting Nazi orders, rebels could endanger the entire community. Nevertheless, a Jewish underground movement grew.

Underground

By early 1940, Mordechai Anielewicz was a full-time activist, setting up not only youth groups but also underground newspapers. The danger involved in these activities cannot be overstated. In Poland as early as October 1939, all publishing had come under German control. The Nazis completely restricted the flow of news and information. They permitted only the Judenrats to retain some small printing equipment. Under these circumstances, the mere dissemination of news—war news; political developments; diplomatic affairs; simple chronicles of events

inside Warsaw, Poland, Europe, or worldwide—
became an act of political opposition.

For Jewish residents of Warsaw and other
areas of the Generalgouvernement, the vehicle
best suited to uphold morale and to spread the
views of political parties was the underground
press. Every social and political movement had

This is the cover of the underground Yiddish
newspaper JugendShtimme ("Voice of the Youth"),
depicting a human fist pounding a swastika,
the notorious symbol of the Nazi Party.

its own newspaper, that was printed, mimeographed, or typewritten in secret. These Jewish underground sheets appeared in Hebrew, Yiddish, and Polish. They also gave each party access to the larger society. Papers not only promoted the beliefs of a group, but also advocated for the oppressed Jews in their struggle for survival. Anti-Nazi editorials in the underground papers articulated the hatred that the silenced populace felt for the Germans.

Anielewicz managed the Hasomer Hatzair newspaper, *Neged Hazerem* ("Against the Stream"). He wrote editorials, and at a conference of Zionist youth, he encouraged the delegates: "Our time will come, but in the interim we must hold out by every and all means." He often printed and distributed appeals to the Jewish people: "Awaken, my people, to the great danger!"

Danger for Jewish activists was ever present—especially for those involved with an underground press. Security in issuing a paper, distributing it, even reading it, became literally a matter of life and death. For purposes of security, underground publishers continually changed their papers' names, hoping to throw the Germans off the track. In her diary, thirteen-year-old Warsaw resident Halina Gorcewicz described the way in which her friend Josek obtained illegal printed materials:

> Another boy sidled up to Josek in the street. They spoke to each other for a moment and then Josek had in his hand a conspiratory pamphlet called "Poland Lives," No. 26. He would not show it to us until we returned home, when all of us read it.

All underground papers devoted most of their space to military and political news regarding the war. The news was gathered from the British Broadcasting Corporation (BBC) radio broadcasts from London and from Russian or underground stations in the occupied territories.

Seeds of Resistance

We, the Jewish youth, can not free ourselves from the influence of the situation as a whole on young people in general. To this is added the specific lack of contact with the land of the Jews and the special hatred that accompanies us as Jews. The war and the Nazi Occupation have revealed the tragedy of our Jewish youth very sharply. We have become a group that is ostracized, attacked, and humiliated, the object of scorn and derision. What must we do in this situation? We must gather together the best of the Jewish youth, which has already received its education in our movement, and forge it into a cadre that is prepared for battle and that will lead the way for Jewish youth.

—From "Jewish Youth at the Present Time," printed in the underground newspaper *Dror* in August 1940

In Poland, the Nazis not only took control of publishing, but also outlawed all political parties. The Gestapo, the special secret police unit of the SS, rounded up dozens of political activists, sometimes incarcerating them in camps, but more often killing them. Flight, arrest, and murder depleted Jewish political leadership from the start of the occupation. However, the left-wing parties and socialist Zionist youth movements succeeded in maintaining their political character and in transforming their prewar organizations into functioning underground organizations

Significantly, in the absence of party veterans, of mature and experienced leaders, young people, like Anielewicz, began to move forward and make their presence felt. Frustration among Jewish youth was mounting. As Nazi plans intensified, so too would the urgency of these calls for resistance.

5. The Warsaw Ghetto

The second period of German rule in Poland was ghettoization. Ghettos were a logical extension of Nazi plans to isolate the Jews. In Warsaw, the imprisonment of Jews within ghetto walls was the end result of a gradual process. Barbed wire enclosed the main streets of the Jewish population as early as October 1939. Soon thereafter, the Germans contemplated introducing a ghetto in Warsaw, but yielded to Jewish protests and postponed the decision.

On November 4, 1939, the SS ordered Adam Czerniakow, chair of the Warsaw Judenrat, to summon all members to an emergency meeting. Judenrat members were met by Gestapo (*Geheime Staatspolizei*, or Secret State Police) officers. Before twenty-four members and twenty-four alternates, a Gestapo officer

read an army decree that ordered all Jews in
Warsaw to move to an area designated as the
Jewish ghetto within three days. All alternate
members were held hostage by armed Gestapo
soldiers. The rest of the Judenrat members were
then warned that these men would be shot if the
Judenrat failed to comply with the order as
specified. For reasons that still remain unclear,
the order was suddenly withdrawn.

In December 1939, the Nazis compelled the
Judenrat to set up large wooden signs, reading
"Danger: Epidemic Zone," at thirty-four street
corners leading into the heart of the Jewish
quarter of Warsaw. Indeed, the area in which the
ghetto was finally established, known as
Seuchensperrgebiet, had once been used to
quarantine epidemics. On October 2, 1940,
German authorities instructed all local leaders
to begin work on the resettlement required for
the establishment of Jewish quarters in Warsaw.
Waldemar Schon, head of the Department of
Resettlement in the Warsaw District, stated the
racist reasons for the resettlement:

1. The German army and population must in any case be protected against the Jews, the immune carriers of the bacteria of epidemics.

2. The separation of the Jews from the rest of the population, both Poles and ethnic Germans (*Volksdeutsche*), is a political and moral requirement. Jewish thinking and action had up to now dominated the population of the eastern lands. The beneficial effects of the elimination of Jewish influence can now already be seen. If the German task of reconstruction is to be successful at all, then the freedom of Jewry to act in the area must be ended.

3. A further reason derives from the need to secure the execution of war economy measures and safeguarding the nutrition level in general by stopping the black market and raising prices.

The Warsaw ghetto was formally and finally introduced on October 16, 1940. Generalgouvernement governor Hans Frank had ordered that the resettlement of Jews into the ghetto be complete by November 15, 1940. On November 16, the entrances to the ghetto were closed.

Red brick walls three meters high and fences of barbed wire separated Jews from all other parts of Warsaw. After being considered second- or third-rate citizens, the Jews were completely segregated from the city and its inhabitants. All of the estimated 400,000 Jews in Warsaw squeezed into the limited space of 100 square city blocks. The ghetto contained only 27,000 apartments, each with an average of only two and a half rooms.

Life in the Ghetto

Ghetto conditions were horrendous. German soldiers constantly harassed ghetto residents for one transgression or another: violating

Jewish youth peer over a wall in the
Warsaw ghetto.

curfew, not wearing armbands, smuggling, leaving the ghetto illegally. Overcrowding caused a breakdown in sanitation. Three and four families lived in a space adequate for one. Toilets, running water, all plumbing, and sewage facilities were taxed beyond capacity and broken beyond repair. Staying warm soon became more important than cleanliness. In mid-November 1941, Emmanuel Ringelblum, ghetto resident and historian, observed in his diary, "The most fearful sight is that of freezing children," standing "dumbly weeping in he street with bare feet, bare knees, and torn clothing."

Adding to the misery, the Germans instituted a policy of starving the Jews. By 1941, the Germans had rationed food supplies in Poland in the following manner: 2,613 calories per day for Germans in Poland, 699 calories per day for Poles, and

184 calories per day for Jews in the ghetto. As one anonymous observer wrote:

We have nothing to eat,
They gave us a turnip; they gave us a beet.
Here have some grub, have some fleas,
Have some typhus, die of disease.

Hunger obsessed everyone; it affected the body and the mind. People began to beg and steal to survive. Only the illegal smuggling of food into the ghetto kept Jews alive.

In fact, smuggling became a big business. It took place through walls and gates, via underground tunnels, through sewers and houses along the ghetto border. Buildings bordering the ghetto, with entrances on the "Aryan" side, became smugglers' nerve centers, operational headquarters for hoisting and lowering. Small cranes, makeshift lifts, troughs, and pipes delivered

The Girl Couriers of the Underground Movement

May 19, 1942

The heroic girls, Chajka Grosman, Frumke Plotnicka and others—theirs is a story that calls for the pen of a great writer. They are venturesome, courageous girls who travel here and there across Poland to cities and towns, carrying Aryan papers which describe them as Polish or Ukrainian. One of them even wears a cross, which she never leaves off and misses when she is in the ghetto. Day by day they face the greatest dangers, relying completely on their Aryan appearance and the kerchiefs they tie around their heads. They accept the most dangerous missions and carry them out without a murmur, without a moment's hesitation. If there is need for someone to travel to Vilna, Bialystok, Lvov, Kowel, Lubin, Czestochowa, or Radom to smuggle in such forbidden things as illegal publications, goods, money, they do it all as though it were the most natural thing. If there are comrades to be rescued from Vilna, Lublin, or other cities, they take the job on themselves. Nothing deters them, nothing stops them. If it is necessary to make friends with the Germans responsible for a train so as to travel beyond the borders of the

Government-General, which is allowed
only for people with special permits—
they do it quite simply, as though it
were their profession. They travel
from city to city, where no
representative of any Jewish
institution has reached, such as
Volhynia and Lithuania. They were the
first to bring the news of the tragedy
in Vilna. They were the first to take
back messages of greeting and
encouragement to the survivors in
Vilna. How many times did they look
death in the eye? How many times were
they arrested and searched? But their
luck held. "Those who go on an errand
of mercy will meet no evil." With what
modesty and simplicity do they deliver
their reports on what they
accomplished during their travels on
trains where Christians, men and
women, were picked up and taken away
for work in Germany. Jewish women have
written a shining page in the history
of the present World War. The Chajkes
and Frumkes will take the first place
in this history. These girls do not
know what it is to rest. They have
hardly arrived from Czestochowa, where
they took forbidden goods, and in a
few hours, they would move on again:
they do it without a moment's
hesitation, and without a
minute's rest.

                    —Emmanuel Ringelblum
    Warsaw ghetto resident and historian

grain, milk, cereal, and vegetables. As
Emmanuel Ringelblum observed:

> Smuggling began at the very moment
> that the Jewish area of residence was
> established . . . Among the Jewish victims

Portrait of Ludzia Hamersztejn, a member of
the Hashomer Hatzair Zionist youth movement
and a former courier for the Jewish underground
in Poland.

of the smuggling there were tens of Jewish children between five and six years old, whom the German killers shot in great numbers near the passages and at the walls . . . And despite that, without paying attention to the victims, the smuggling never stopped for a moment.

If not for the smugglers, the Germans would have succeeded in starving to death the people in the ghetto.

Jews employed other strategies of survival. In addition to smuggling, neighbors developed informational networks. For example, ghetto Jews evaded forced labor by setting up human cooperative security systems within buildings to warn of imminent seizures.

The bleak physical conditions of the ghetto also caused severe psychological distress for its residents. One of the very purposes of the ghetto was to lower Jewish morale. The hideous conditions within the ghetto not only weakened bodies, but also dimmed spirits.

> Everything taking place outside the ghetto walls became more and more foggy, distant, strange. Only the present day really mattered. Only matters of the most personal nature, the closest circle of friends were by now the focal point of interest to the average ghetto inhabitant. The most important thing was simply "to be alive."
> —Marek Edelman, subcommander of ghetto forces, who would later retaliate against the Nazis

"To Be Alive"

Initially, many ghetto inhabitants favored finding a way to make the best of a bad situation. These people believed that the Allied forces would soon defeat the Nazis, and therefore considered patience the key to survival. The most important thing was to stay put and try to save what remained. Many Jews in the ghetto felt that they had to come to terms with their imprisonment. That realization was not the result of passive resignation, but one of strategically trying to endure, hang onto hope, and cling to life until their hideous nightmare ended.

Those Jews who considered the preservation of life to be their ultimate goal employed tactics of accommodation and adaptability. For many, survival itself constituted an act of defiance. One elderly man with no family, who would seem to have nothing to live for, was noted as saying, "I want to see the end of the war, even if I live only another half an hour!"

Ghetto streets only became bloodier. The Germans made a habit of shooting passersby without the slightest provocation. People tried to avoid trouble by staying inside, but the Germans also shot into homes. Many in the ghetto were stunned by the severity of what was happening to them. The German and Jewish police constantly hunted Jews on the streets and sent captives to Nazi labor camps.

In fact, the German demand for Jewish labor convinced some Jews that ultimately the Germans had an interest in keeping Jews alive. Some Jews reasoned that the Germans were more interested in increasing their wartime productive power and enslaving Jews as laborers. Although many Jews understood that conditions in the labor camps were difficult, they believed that work in these camps provided them with an opportunity to live through the war. This line of thinking also helped convince some Jews that protest and resistance activities were misguided. Consequently, plans for full-scale armed resistance in the Warsaw ghetto remained dormant. But, the escalation of Nazi plans would soon spur many ghetto residents to take up arms.

6. Deportations

By the summer of 1941, the Nazis had murdered about one million European Jews. Nevertheless, the Nazi leadership considered the methods employed up to that point—mass shooting, starvation, and slave labor—relatively ineffective. Instead, they developed a systematic genocide plan. The Nazis decided to construct killing centers in occupied Poland, to transport all remaining Jews under German control in Europe to these death camps, and to kill them with poisonous gas.

On July 31, 1941, Hermann Göring, a leader of the Nazi Party who had overseen the creation of the Nazi police state in Germany, ordered Reinhard Heydrich to prepare a plan for the "Final Solution of the Jewish Problem." Heydrich presented his plan to thirteen state

and party leaders on January 20, 1942, at the
Wannsee Conference hall in suburban Berlin.
Hitler's select corps, the SS, especially the
Einsatzgruppen, would implement the Final
Solution, running the work and extermination
camps. The Germans eventually built or
modified six extermination camps: Auschwitz,
Belzec, Chelmno, Lublin-Majdanek, Sobibor,
and Treblinka.

The Nazis first experimented with mobile
gassing units, which killed Jews from poisoning,
but they eventually installed permanent gas
chambers and crematoria, where bodies would
be burned. The gas chambers in five camps
used carbon monoxide. In Auschwitz, the gas
used was hydrogen cyanide or prussic acid—
known commercially as Zyklon B.

Deportations, or the forced movement of
Jews, began in September 1941. Initially,
deportations involved the transportation of
Jews from Germany and Austria to the death
camps. However, the killing centers were not
yet complete, so the Nazis imprisoned their

The rear side of the gas chamber in Lublin-Majdanck. The furnace on the right was used to create carbon monoxide for gassing prisoners.

victims in overcrowded ghettos close to the death camps, to await transport to their final destination. By the end of 1941, the construction of the Chelmno death camps was complete and it became operational.

The Nazis kept their plans highly classified. To this end, they clothed their vile plans in vague language, attempting to mask their genocidal intentions. Rather than planning

Such was life in the ghetto when the first report of the gassing of the Jews in Chelmno reached Warsaw. The news was brought by three persons who were to be put to death in Chelmno and had miraculously escaped. The Warsaw ghetto did not believe these reports. People who clung to their lives with superhuman determination were unable to believe that they could be killed in such a manner. Only our organized youth groups, carefully noting the steadily increasing signs of German terror, accepted the Chelmno story as indeed probable, and decided upon extensive propaganda activities in order to inform the population of the imminent danger.

—Marek Edelman

"murder" or "genocide," many party officials spoke of "cleansing Europe" or "handling the Jewish problem." Consequently, few people inside or outside of Europe believed the initial reports of death camps and mass killings.

The extent to which Jews within the Warsaw ghetto understood Nazi plans for genocide and knew of plans to create death camps varies. An important part of Nazi strategy was to stem the flow of information into the ghetto. Nevertheless, reports from prisoners who had escaped from the death camps trickled in through cracks in the ghetto walls. When news reached Warsaw, the horror described seemed unreal. Many continued to consider Jewish deaths the result of individual acts of wartime violence. For many, the idea of an organized policy to exterminate the Jewish people still seemed unfathomable.

On the Alert

Young people who had been active in the Zionist and other youth organizations prior to World War II spearheaded efforts to organize resistance to deportations in the Warsaw ghetto. Members of these often politically diverse groups, like Marek Edelman and Anielewicz, had long been engaged in combating a common foe: anti-Semitism. Faced with the gruesome and terrifying accounts of labor camps and death camps related by escaped prisoners, Anielewicz began concentrating on alerting ghetto inhabitants. He actively encouraged Jews in the Warsaw ghetto to resist deportation to these camps. Anielewicz also turned his focus to uniting the several underground youth movements into a single armed resistance movement.

Jewish resistance fighters hide in a crowded bunker after escaping the Warsaw ghetto uprising and liquidation by the SS.

Many leaders in the ghetto had already recognized the need to address the particular sufferings and frustrations of young people in the Warsaw ghetto. In 1941, a committee of resistance leaders within the ghetto established a youth division and offered young people an opportunity to participate in activities ranging from choir practice to education and political planning.

While conditions for Jews in the Warsaw ghetto were horrendous, Jewish youth suffered particular tortures. German soldiers persecuted Jewish youth with special cruelty, especially young men, whom they continuously hunted to serve in forced labor camps. Within the ghetto, young men and women rarely felt free to walk the streets, let alone attempt regular work.

At this point, the goal of the Youth Division, for Anielewicz and other leaders, was to remedy the degradation of the young first and foremost through education. Anielewicz's organizational activities also extended outside the Warsaw ghetto. Exhibiting amazing bravery, Anielewicz risked death, sneaking in and out of the ghetto to respond to people in need, helping organize resistance in communities outside of Warsaw.

Anielewicz worked within an underground network attempting to evade and thwart the Nazis. This network succeeded in a variety of ways, from smuggling food into the ghetto and falsifying identity papers to helping Jews escape from Poland and spreading important information regarding Nazi tactics. People working for the underground literally risked their lives to save the lives of others.

Weapons

It soon became clear to Anielewicz and other resistance leaders that they needed to embrace the idea of armed resistance, but obtaining weapons proved to be quite difficult. Like most things of use to ghetto residents, arms were smuggled in using hazardous tactics. During one smuggling mission Edzia Pesahzon, a fellow member of Hashomer Hatzair, fell into German hands. The Germans discovered the weapons she was carrying. In an attempt to extract information, the Germans tortured her but she said nothing.

In the spring of 1942, the Germans carried out mass arrests of Jews in ghettos throughout Poland. These particular actions seemed directed against political activists, although the pattern was not consistent. In Warsaw, beginning late on Friday, April 17, and long into the next morning, the Gestapo seized fifty Jews in their homes and shot them on the street. Most of those rounded up were printers and persons associated with the underground press. That night became known as Bloody Friday.

For many ghetto inhabitants, Bloody Friday became a turning point. Many who, until that time, had tried to believe they could endure the wrath of the Germans began to understand that the Nazis intended to destroy the ghetto. Still, few realized that the Nazis intended to kill the entire Jewish population.

Aktion

July 22, 1942, marked the first phase of deportations from the Warsaw ghetto. At 10 AM members of the *Umsiedlungskommando,* or German Deportation Board, arrived at the Jewish Council buildings. During a short meeting with the members of the Warsaw Judenrat, the Germans ordered the deportation of all "unproductive" Jews. Only those engaged in what German military authorities designated as essential war production were exempt from deportation. While the Nazis claimed they were sending deportees somewhere to the East, in truth, the Nazis deported Jews from Warsaw to the Treblinka camp.

As soon as the deportations began, ghetto activists attempted to consolidate the political underground and devise a resistance strategy. They failed. As a consequence, a meeting was held on July 28 among representatives of three movements, including Hashomer Hatzair. At this meeting, they began to establish a Jewish fighting organization and so the Jewish Combat Organization, or ZOB, was born.

Those in command of the organization sent emissaries to the Aryan side of Warsaw in order to establish contact with the Polish underground and obtain weapons by any possible means. Despite continuous efforts, weapons remained elusive. When members of the newly formed ZOB finally secured a few revolvers and hand grenades, they were discovered by the Nazis. As a result, the Germans murdered two members of the ZOB command, Yosef Kaplan and Shmuel Braslaw.

At the height of the deportation, often referred to as the *Aktion* by ghetto residents, the ghetto fighters had engaged in feverish attempts to survive and save their families. When this period of deportations ended, survivors began to suffer feelings of sorrow and guilt at the loss of loved ones. As one ghetto resident observed, this sorrow soon transformed into rage. "Husbands tore out their hair because they had let the Germans, unharmed, take away those dearest to them. Oaths were sworn aloud: Never shall the Germans move us from here with impunity; we will die, but the cruel invaders will pay with their blood for ours."

The deportations continued into September, resulting in the transfer of 254,000 Jews to the Treblinka death camp and 11,000 Jews to labor camps. Despite failures and setbacks, the ZOB had succeeded in protecting a considerable portion of its members. By the time the deportations ceased on September 21, 1942, the ZOB had at its disposal a sizeable group of highly motivated fighters.

By late 1942, all involved in the Jewish political underground, young activists as well as community elders, had come to see that German atrocities against the Jews were not simply the result of Hitler's war against Allied forces but part of a deliberate design to destroy the Jews. Only 60,000 Jews remained in the ghetto, of whom some 25,000 remained in hiding. Most realized that the deportations would continue; it was only a matter of time.

The Nazis had hoped to destroy all Polish ghettos by the end of 1942. Heinrich Himmler outlined their plans:

> I herewith order that the resettlement of the entire Jewish population of the Government-General be carried out and completed by December 31, 1942 . . . These measures are required with a view to the necessary ethnic division of races and peoples for the New Order in Europe, and also in the interests of the security and cleanliness of the German Reich and its sphere of interest.

As it turned out, the process took somewhat longer. In March 1943, the Kracow ghetto was liquidated; the Germans had deported all of its residents to camps. In April, the Germans attempted to deport the remaining Jews in the Warsaw ghetto. To their surprise, the Jews retaliated.

7. The First Uprising

The first phase of deportations had devastated the Warsaw ghetto. New walls divided the ghetto and between the inhabited blocks there were vast, desolate areas. The stench of unburied dead bodies hung in the air.

Ghetto residents remained tense and ghetto conditions continued to deteriorate. Many Jews hid out in cellars and underground shelters or bunkers. Food continued to be scarce. Tuberculosis and typhus were rampant.

Of those Jews not in hiding, 3,000 were employees of the Jewish Council. Over 30,000 Jews continued to work in factories and for German employers. The Germans exploited the lives of those they spared. Workers of one shop were forbidden to communicate with those of another. Workdays were at least twelve hours long.

The mood of grief and the desire for revenge provided the impetus for the expansion and consolidation of the Jewish fighting organization, the ZOB. In October 1942, talks between several resistance groups began with the intention of coordinating their efforts. They decided that a joint battle organization should be formed with the purpose of preparing for another round of German deportations. Soon thereafter, representatives from these talks appointed Mordechai Anielewicz commander of the newly enlarged ZOB.

At this point, the ghetto was comprised of three areas. Anielewicz and the ZOB organized their efforts accordingly. They formed several battle groups within each section. A major problem that had plagued resistance efforts within the ghetto since its formation was the lack of weapons.

The ZOB continued to appeal to the non-Jewish Polish resistance movement. For a number of reasons, the Polish resistance was initially slow to provide the ghetto with underground support. Lingering anti-Semitism was at least partly responsible for inhibiting the coordination of resistance efforts; many in the Polish underground remained skeptical that the Jews would indeed fight the Nazis. Also, the Polish underground grappled with many of the

A Jewish man emerges from his hiding place below the floor of a bunker, prepared for the Warsaw ghetto uprising.

same constraints that the ghetto underground did: difficulty organizing, limited resources, and a scarcity of weapons. Finally, at the end of December 1942, the ZOB received its first, if small, transport of weapons from the Polish underground.

A Taste of Victory

On January 18, 1943, the Germans launched the second mass deportation from the Warsaw ghetto. Caught by surprise, the ZOB staff did not have time to communicate. While the ZOB knew that deportations would resume, they had not anticipated the timing. Different sections of the ghetto responded in varying ways. A group commanded by Mordechai Anielewicz and armed with revolvers deliberately joined a large convoy of Jews being taken to the central square for deportation. Close to the site, on a given signal, they broke out of line and commenced hand-to-hand combat with the German soldiers escorting the convoy.

Most of them fell fighting. Miraculously, Mordechai Anielewicz survived. Led by Anielewicz's second-in-command, Yitzhak Zuckerman, other groups engaged in armed combat inside a ghetto building. This form of combat proved more suitable than street battle in clashes between such uneven forces; it was adopted as the basic combat method of the ZOB.

Four days later, the Germans halted the deportations. The ZOB knew that, although they had temporarily stopped the deportations, there would be further fighting. The ZOB prepared intensively for the next conflict.

The events that began on January 18, 1943, constituted a decisive turning point that, more than any other occurrence, shaped the scope and character of the final uprising in April. The use of firearms by Jews and the losses inflicted on the Germans came as a stunning shock to those both inside and outside of the ghetto. As ZOB member Marek Edelman recalled:

These partisans from Warsaw were part of
Mordechai Anielewicz's fighting unit.

For now, for the first time, German plans were frustrated. For the first time the halo of omnipotence and invincibility was torn from the Germans' heads. For the first time the Jew in the street realized that it was possible to do something against the Germans' will and power. The number of Germans killed by ZOB bullets was not the only important thing. What was more important was the appearance of a psychological turning point. The mere fact that because of the unexpected resistance, weak as it was, the Germans were forced to interrupt their "deportation" schedule was of great value.

The attitude of the Polish underground had also changed after the armed uprising in January 1943. They could no longer claim that the Jews would never fight. They supplied a few more weapons as well as military instruction. However, they also tried to curb Jewish militancy. The Polish underground feared that the revolt in the ghetto might break out at an inconvenient time for them. They preferred to conserve their efforts until it was possible to direct their attacks against both German and Russian forces.

ZOB Plans

The ZOB used the three months between January and April to intensively train the fighting forces, acquire weapons, and draw up a strategic plan for the defense of the ghetto. At this point, the ghetto fully supported the ZOB. Arms were smuggled in; bribed Polish and Jewish police officers looked the other way. After importing the necessary ingredients into the ghetto, the ZOB set up a factory for the production of hand grenades and Molotov cocktails, which consisted of bottles or other breakable containers filled with flammable liquid and a lighting mechanism.

In many ways, the ZOB ruled the ghetto. During this time, the ZOB actively sought out and killed any individuals collaborating with the Germans, especially Jewish Gestapo agents. Their forces also attempted to protect workers from German violence and harassment. The Germans and the ZOB waged a war of propaganda in the ghetto. The Germans tried to convince the Jews that deportation only meant being transported to labor camps. They falsely promised that the Jews could live out the war in peace. The ZOB knew otherwise.

8. The Final Uprising

On April 19, 1943, the Germans resumed the deportations of Jews in the Warsaw ghetto. Strategically, they had chosen the eve of Passover, a sacred Jewish holiday celebrated each spring to commemorate the liberation of the Israelites from enslavement in ancient Egypt. As the Germans again called for Jews to report for deportation to so-called labor camps, death seemed imminent.

The first round of deportations in the summer of 1942 had emptied a large portion of the ghetto. In January 1943, the ZOB had managed to disrupt another attempt by the Germans to resume deportations, but only temporarily. This round of deportations, the Jews knew, represented the final attempt by the Nazis to empty and destroy the Warsaw ghetto. As a result, only a small number of ghetto inhabitants responded to the summons to report for deportation.

Up to this point, *Obergruppenführer* Ferdinand von Sammern-Frankenegg was the chief of the SS and police in the Warsaw district. Undoubtedly Sammern-Frankenegg was aware of the existence of a Jewish defense organization, but he apparently did not dare

An SS soldier stands among ruins in the Warsaw ghetto during the suppression of the uprising.

admit this to his superiors. The fact that the starving, disease-ridden, downtrodden ghetto population had formed a fighting force that was willing to stand up to the seemingly all-powerful Nazi forces made Sammern-Frankenegg look weak and ineffectual.

Heinrich Himmler, a shrewd military leader, did not rely on the reports of Sammern-Frankenegg. On the eve of the final deportation, Himmler replaced Sammern-Frankenegg with General Jurgen Stroop, an SS member and police commander who had experience fighting partisans and street fighters. As leader of German forces in Warsaw, his task was to suppress any uprising and bring the ghetto to its knees.

Through the Polish underground, ghetto fighters had received advance knowledge of the timing of the final deportation. At this point, most ghetto fighters were equipped with one pistol, four to five hand grenades, and four to five Molotov cocktails. The ZOB dispersed a small number of rifles and machine guns.

On April 19 at 2:00 AM, the Germans, aided by Polish police, approached the ghetto. The ZOB was alerted. Fifteen minutes later, all ZOB groups waited at designated battle stations. By refusing to comply with the Germans' orders to report for deportation, all ghetto residents became part of the uprising. The ZOB warned residents about the invasion and most moved quickly to previously-prepared shelters and hideouts in the cellars and attics of buildings. The streets were empty; the ghetto was silent.

Before Dawn

In the hours before dawn, the Germans entered the ghetto in small groups, in the hope that they would not arouse suspicion. By early morning, a number of German tanks and army vehicles roared into the ghetto. The Nazi soldiers closed into formation and began to march in the streets. The ghetto, so still and so silent, had fooled the Nazis into believing that ZOB forces had run in fear.

But as soon as the Germans began to set up camp within a street intersection, ZOB fighters opened fire. The battle groups threw their homemade hand grenades and shot their guns and rifles. At the same time, battles began in other areas of the ghetto. By that afternoon, the Germans had retreated out of the ghetto and ZOB forces had succeeded in capturing a few Nazi weapons, including machine guns.

The Germans tried again, attempting to enter the ghetto through several different locations. At each, they encountered resistance. Every house and building was a fortress. The Germans could not capture Jewish fighters, who after every clash managed to retreat by way of rooftops. Nor could the Germans lay hands on the Jews hiding in the bunkers. One ZOB commander described these guerilla tactics that initially stymied Nazi forces. "At the second story window is Dwojra, firing away rancorously [angrily]. The Germans spot her: '*Schau,*

From Mordechai Anielewicz,
dated April 23, 1943:

It is impossible to put into
words what we have been through.
One thing is clear, what happened
exceeded our boldest dreams. The
Germans ran twice from the
ghetto. One of our companies held
out for forty minutes and another
for more than six hours. The mine
set in the "brushmakers" area
exploded. Several of our companies
attacked the dispersing Germans.
Our losses in manpower are
minimal. That is also an
achievement. Y Yechiel fell. He
fell a hero, at the machine gun.
I feel that great things are
happening and what we dared do is
of great, enormous importance.

   Beginning from today we shall
shift over to the partisan
tactic. Three battle companies
will move out tonight, with two
tasks: reconnaissance and
obtaining arms. Do you remember,
short-range weapons are of no use
to us. We use such weapons only
rarely. What we need urgently:
grenades, rifles, machine guns
and explosives.

It is impossible to
describe the conditions under
which the Jews of the ghetto
are now living. Only a few will
be able to hold out. The
remainder will die sooner or
later. Their fate is decided.
In almost all the hiding
places in which thousands are
concealing themselves it is not
possible to light a candle for
lack of air.

With the aid of our
transmitter we heard a
marvelous report on our
fighting by the "Shavit" radio
station. The fact that we are
remembered beyond the ghetto
walls encourages us in our
struggle. Peace go with you, my
friend! Perhaps we may still
meet again! The dream of my
life has risen to become fact.
Self-defense in the ghetto will
have been a reality. Jewish
armed resistance and revenge
are facts. I have been a
witness to the magnificent,
heroic fighting of Jewish men
and women of battle.

Hans, eine Frau schiesst!' [Look, Hans, a woman shoots!] They try to get her, but somehow their bullets miss. She, apparently, does not miss often, for, strangely enough, they withdraw quickly."

Initially, the Jewish resistance fighters held the upper hand, and the Germans suffered losses. Street fighting continued. Time and again, General Stroop claimed in his daily reports that he had overcome ZOB forces. Stroop also claimed that the uprising was dying out, only to report the next day that there was no end to the attacks and the losses suffered by his troops. In spite of the fighters' stubborn persistence and daring, the losses they inflicted on the Germans remained small. Their lack of weapons continued to hinder their efforts.

A New German Strategy

The Germans decided to abandon ordinary fighting methods. Their new plan: Set the ghetto on fire. Building by building, they would systematically burn the ghetto. In this way, fighters and residents hiding within the buildings would either die in the flames or escape into the street, only to face the wrath of the German army. This forced the ZOB to shift their strategy as well. Rather than fight at length in the street, they staged sporadic raids against the Nazis.

Battles continued. They were now fought mostly at night, in complete darkness. An unsettling quiet blanketed the ghetto during daylight. As the Germans continued to burn the ghetto, hiding and living quarters became scarce. Fighters sought refuge in underground shelters along with civilians. The situation soon turned grave. Food, water, and ammunition became scarce. As the street fighting ended and the Germans introduced a large military force against a few hundred Jewish fighters, Anielewicz and some of his staff retreated into a bunker, ZOB headquarters, at 18 Mila Street.

On May 8, the Germans surrounded ZOB headquarters. Mordechai Anielewicz and a large group of fighters and commanders battled the Germans for two hours. When the Germans realized they could not take the bunker, they threw a gas bomb into it. According to one account, "Whoever survived the German bullets, whoever was not gassed, committed suicide, for it was quite clear that from here there was no way out, and nobody even considered being taken alive by the Germans."

The ZOB fighters had not made any elaborate plans for a retreat from the ghetto, their assumption being that the battle would go on inside the ghetto until the last fighter had fallen. Some ZOB members did manage to escape from the ghetto through the sewers.

On May 16, General Stroop announced that the fighting was over and that "we succeeded in capturing altogether 56,065 Jews, that is, definitely destroying them." Stroop then planned to blow up the Great Synagogue on

SS troops guard members of the Jewish resistance
captured during the suppression of the Warsaw
ghetto uprising.

Tlomack Street (which was outside the ghetto and the scene of the fighting) as a symbol of victory and celebration of the fact that the Jewish quarter of Warsaw no longer existed.

While German forces defeated the ZOB, Warsaw was ultimately liberated by Allied forces in January, 1945. The last German forces were finally expelled from Poland in the spring of 1945. When the war ended, close to 70,000 Polish Jews were found to have survived in Poland, in the Polish army, and in camps in Germany. Further, some 200,000 Polish Jews had survived in Russia. Three million Polish Jews were dead. Counted among them were Mordechai Anielewicz and the ghetto fighters.

These men and women died refusing to accept a fate planned by the Nazis. Their vigilance was breathtaking, their deaths heartbreaking. Yet, it is important to remember that they were not the only Jewish warriors. All Jews who faced Hitler's wrath engaged in battle, the battle to survive. Hoping to outlast the nightmare their lives had become, some focused on the fundamentals of survival. Others resisted with arms. The goal for all was to carry on a Jewish legacy.

Because the Nazis crushed the ghetto uprising, it would be easy to regard Anielewicz's mission as the spark that failed to fully ignite. But that would imply that the freedom fighters died in vain. Their lives and their deaths speak otherwise. The story of Mordechai Anielewicz and the ZOB adds another layer to the history of the Holocaust, revealing the political and cultural vitality within the Jewish community during World War II. In this way, they triumphed and for this reason, theirs is a story we must never forget.

Timeline

1919   Mordechai Anielewicz is born in
                         Warsaw, Poland.

September 1939   Hitler invades Poland and divides the
                         country into three major areas. The
                         central portion became a German
                         protectorate known as the
                         Generalgouvernement.

November 1939   Governor Frank issues anti-Jewish
                         measures, including the mandate that
                         Jews must wear identifying armbands.
                         Governor Frank issues a decree
                         ordering the formation of a *Judenrat,*
                         or Jewish council.

October 1940   The Warsaw ghetto is built. Jews are
                         sealed inside, separated from the rest of
                         the city and its inhabitants.

December 1941 Chelmno becomes the first death camp to become operational.

July- December 1942 Over 300,000 Jews are deported from the Warsaw ghetto to the Treblinka death camp.

October 1942 Representatives of the Jewish Combat Organization (ZOB) appoint Mordechai Anielewicz commander.

April 1943 German attempts to liquidate the Warsaw ghetto meet with armed resistance.

May 1943 Mordechai Anielewicz dies during the Warsaw ghetto uprising.

Glossary

Allied Forces
In World War II, Great Britain, France, the Soviet
   Union, and (after 1941) the United States.

Aryan
In Nazi ideology, a race that was destined to rule and
   enslave inferior races.

Führer
German word for "leader," Adolf Hitler's title as
   dictator of Germany.

genocide
The systematic killing of an entire ethnic, racial, or
   cultural group.

Gestapo
Nazi secret state police, established in 1933.

ghetto
A sealed-off area where Jews were forced to live.

Holocaust
The murder of six million Jews by Nazi Germany during World War II.

Judenrat
Jewish councils, established by the Nazis to enforce Nazi orders.

Nazi Party
The National Socialist German Workers' Party, which came to power in Germany and was headed by Adolf Hitler.

partisans
Members of small groups that tried to resist the Nazis.

pogrom
An assault against Jews or other minorities, sometimes sanctioned by local leaders.

protectorate
An area governed by an authority.

reparations
Payments made by countries who have lost a war to the victors.

secularization
To become more worldly and not overtly or specifically religious.

Schutzstaffel (SS)
Hitler's select corps of Nazi troops.

Sicherheitsdienst (SD)
The secret police division of the SS.

Third Reich
The title of Hitler's reign with the Nazis in Germany from 1933 through 1945.

Treaty of Versailles
The treaty that ended World War I and forced Germany to pay the victors sizeable reparations.

Zionism
A movement of European Jews that called for the return of Jews to the land of Palestine and the establishment of a Jewish state.

ZOB
The Jewish Combat Organization, established in the Warsaw ghetto. The ZOB spearheaded the Warsaw ghetto uprising.

For More Information

Organizations

The Center for Holocaust and Genocide Studies
University of Minnesota
100 Nolte Hall West
315 Pillsbury Drive
Minneapolis, MN 55455
email: chgs@tc.umn.edu
Web site: http://www.chgs.umn.edu

Holocaust Teacher Resource Center
P.O. Box 6153
Newport News, VA 23606-6153
e-mail: info@holocaust-trc.org
Web site: http://www.holocaust-trc.org

Museum of Jewish Heritage: A Living Memorial to
     the Holocaust
18 First Place
Battery Park City
New York, NY 10004-1484
(212) 509-6130
Web site: http://www.mjhnyc.org/home.htm

Simon Wiesenthal Center and Museum
   of Tolerance
9786 West Pico Boulevard
Los Angeles, CA 90035
(800) 900-9036
Web site: http://www.wiesenthal .com

United States Holocaust Memorial Museum
100 Raoul Wallenberg Place SW
Washington, DC 20024-2126
(202) 488-0400
Web site: http://www.ushmm.org

Web Sites

Cybrary of the Holocaust
http://www.remember.org

Holocaust Chronicle
http://www.holocaustchronicle.org

Simon Wiesenthal Center Museum of
   Tolerance Online
http://www.wiesenthal.com/mot

A Teacher's Guide to the Holocaust
http://fcit.coedu.usf.edu/holocaust

For Further Reading

Altshuler, David A. *Hitler's War Against the Jews: A Young Reader's Version of the War Against the Jews 1933–1945.* New York: Behrman House, 1978.

Bauer, Yehuda, and Nili Keren. *A History of the Holocaust.* Rev. ed. New York: Franklin Watts, 2001.

Boas, Jacob, ed. *We are Witnesses.* New York: Henry Holt and Company, 1995.

Gilbert, Martin. *The Holocaust: A History of the Jews of Europe during the Second World War.* New York: Henry Holt and Company, 1986.

Hilberg, Raul. *Perpetrators, Victims, Bystanders: The Jewish Catastrophe, 1933–1945.* New York: Aaron Asher Books, 1992.

Meed, Vladka. *On Both Sides of the Wall.* New York: Holocaust Library, 1979.

Rothchild, Sylvia, ed. *Voices From the Holocaust.* New York: New American Library, 1982.

Yahil, Leni. *The Holocaust: The Fate of European Jewry, 1932–1945.* New York: Oxford University Press, 1990.

Zar, Rose. *In the Mouth of the Wolf.* Philadelphia, PA: Jewish Publication Society of America, 1983.

Index

A
Anielewicz, Mordechai, 5–6,
    9–10, 101
  as activist, 47, 71–74
  as commander of ZOB, 81,
    83–84, 94
  as community leader, 40
  death, 10, 97–98, 100
  early days, 13, 17, 19, 21–23
  in his own words, 5, 94–95
anti-Semitism, 9, 13–14, 16–17, 23,
    40, 71, 82

B
Bloody Friday, 75

C
Chelmno death camp, 68–70
concentration/death camps, 7, 10
    67–71, 76, 78, 89
Czerniakow, Adam, 53

E
Edelman, Marek, 70, 71, 84, 86
Einsatzgruppen, 36, 68
Eretz Yisra'el, 17, 41

F
Final Solution, 35, 67–68
Frank, Hans, 32, 38, 42, 56

G
Generalgouvernement, 31–32, 34,
    38, 48, 61
genocide, 7, 8, 34, 69–70
German army, 23, 25, 29, 33, 34, 36,
    87, 91
Germany/Third Reich, 24, 26, 29,
    31, 32, 42, 79
Gestapo, 52, 53–54, 88
Göring, Hermann, 67
Grosman, Chajka, 60–61

H
Hashomer Hatzair, 19–22, 23, 40,
    49, 75, 76
Heydrich, Reinhard, 34–35, 36,
    67–68
Himmler, Heinrich, 32, 33, 34, 36,
    79, 91
Hindenburg, Paul von, 24
Hitler, Adolf, 7, 23, 24, 27–30, 32, 33
  plan to annihiliate the Jews, 8,
    23, 30, 31, 34–36
  racist beliefs, 7, 23–24, 27–30
Holocaust, 6, 7, 10

J
Jewish Combat Organization,
    (ZOB), 10, 77–78, 81, 83–84,
    86–88, 89, 90–96, 97–98, 100
Jewish national state, 17–18, 21

Index

Jewish resistance/underground, 6–7, 9, 10, 41, 46–47, 48–50, 51, 52, 60–61, 63, 65, 66, 73–74, 76, 78, 81
  armed resistance, 66, 72, 74, 77, 81–84, 86–88, 91–97, 101
Jewish youth groups, 70, 71, 72
Jews
  attempt to survive, 8, 9, 64–65, 70, 100–101
  culture and religion, 6, 16, 17, 18, 19, 39–40, 98, 101
  deportation of, 10, 32, 36, 67, 68–69, 71–72, 76
  ghettoization of, 53–56, 69
  how they viewed the Nazis' intent, 9, 49, 65–66, 70, 75, 78, 88
  isolation/segregation of, 7, 8, 37–38
  laws against, 14, 38–39, 46
  murder of, 7–8, 9, 23, 39, 40, 44, 46, 52, 65, 67, 68, 78
  in Poland before Nazis, 13–16
  secular and political life, 16–22, 48–49, 52, 101
  who survived in Poland, 100
Judenrat, 42–46, 47, 53–54, 76

N

Nazi Party, 6, 7, 23, 25, 26, 27, 32, 33, 44, 47
  actions against Jews, 36–41, 42–46, 52, 53–56, 58–59, 63, 65, 77, 88
  plan to annihilate the Jews, 34–36, 38, 67, 69, 70–71, 75, 78–79
  racist policies/ideas, 7–8, 23–24, 27–30, 33, 34, 36, 41, 54–55
newspapers/press, underground, 47–50

P

Palestine, 17, 22
pogroms, 9, 14, 40
Poland
  execution of non-Jewish Poles, 33–34
  invasion of, 8, 23, 30, 32, 33, 34
  occupation of, 11, 36, 51, 52
Polish resistance, 23, 77, 81–83, 86–87, 91

R

Ringelblum, Emmanuel, 58–63
Russia/Soviet Union, 11, 23, 31, 50, 87

S

Schutzstaffel (SS), 31–32, 44, 52, 68, 90, 91
Stroop, Jurgen, 91, 96, 98

T

Treaty of Versailles/Paris peace agreement, 11, 24, 26
Treblinka death camp, 76, 78

W

Wannsee Conference, 68
Warsaw ghetto, 8, 10, 53–56, 75
  deportations from, 76–79, 80, 83–84, 86, 88, 89–91
  life in, 56–59, 63–64, 65–66, 70–71, 73, 80
  smuggling in, 59–63, 74
  uprising, 6, 9, 10
  young people in, 73
World War I, 21, 24, 26

Z

Zionism, 17–22, 41, 49, 52

About the Author
Kerry P. Callahan is an editor and freelance writer living in New York City.

Acknowledgments
Special thanks to Dr. Natalia Aleksiun.

Photo Credits
Cover photo, pp. 20, 25, 28, 33, 39, 44, 48, 57, 62, 69, 72, 82, 90, 99 © USHMM Photo Archives; p. 4 © adapted from map by William L. Nelson, "The Holocaust Encyclopedia," Yale University Press; p. 12 © Archive Photos; p. 85 © Yad Vashem Jerusalem.

Layout
Nelson Sa